Bridgette Bastien

Overcomer

PRAYER Saved My Life
A SERIES BY **Bridgette Bastien**

Overcomer

Scripture quotations from The Authorized (King James) Version. Rights in the Authorized Version in the United Kingdom are vested in the Crown. Reproduced by permission of the Crown's patentee, Cambridge University Press.

Scripture taken from the New King James Version®. Copyright © 1982 by Thomas Nelson. Used by permission. All rights reserved.

All the stories related in this book are true, but most of the names have been changed or omitted to protect the privacy of the people mentioned.

Grateful to **Ajok Deng** (model on the cover) for sharing her natural beauty with the world.

Book cover and select interior page elements designed by **Nicole Lavoie** of **Just Saying Designs**.

Overcomer: Prayer Saved My Life
Copyright ©2019 Bridgette Bastien. All rights reserved.
This book or any portion thereof may not be reproduced or used in any manner whatsoever without the express written permission of the author(s) or publisher except for the use of brief quotations in a book review.
ISBN-13: 978-1-7328798-1-2
ISBN-10: 1-7328798-1-8

Bridgette Bastien

"An *Overcomer* defies all odds by God's grace and prevails over opposition, temptations, addiction, injustice, illness, and fear."

- Bridgette Bastien

Dedication

Thank you to the prayer
warriors in my life –
especially my grandmother,
Catlin Berbeck, a spiritual
rock who happily spends
hours in prayer each day.
You inspire me to be more
like Christ.

I love you with
my whole heart.

Table of Contents

Foreword..i

Author's Preface..iv

Chapter 1: No Time To Pray......................................1

Chapter 2: Don't Remove Prayer..............................9

Chapter 3: Underwater Prayer................................17

Chapter 4: United Prayer..24

Chapter 5: Teacup Prayer.......................................31

Chapter 6: Punk Rock Prayer.................................40

Chapter 7: Red Dress Prayer..................................49

Chapter 8: Prayer Conquers Fear..........................56

Chapter 9: Breakthrough Prayer............................64

Chapter 10: Praying Through Scriptures...............73

Closing Thoughts..82

Foreword

When you or I open a book, any book, and more relevantly, as we open this book about the dynamic power of prayer, there are two important questions that must be answered. First, what's this book about? Secondly, how will you and I benefit from what we read in this book?

Allow me to say that Bridgette Bastien has directly answered the first question by stating her purpose for writing this book on the life changing power of prayer, namely, "to make it into heaven and to help others get there also." That is what prayer is designed to do. Like Enoch, who walked with God through intimate life changing prayer, we too must walk with God in prayer, whilst on this earth, so we can make it into heaven.

This book is about us walking so close to God, that one day like Enoch, so to speak, we will ultimately walk right into heaven when Jesus comes again. Every sin we overcome through prayer, every temptation we resist through prayer, every victory we achieve over self, the devil, and the world, through mighty prevailing prayer, gets us a step closer to that final goal—heaven. For that very reason this book, *Overcomer* is worth every moment of my time and your time.

The answer to the second question will depend much more on you and me. What, for example, are we willing or not willing to do with the life-changing call to transformative prayer in every aspect of our life experiences? Are we willing to spend quality time in prayer and praise to God because He is worthy of it, even if we do not see the answer to our prayer requests from Him?

As the author entreats us, are we willing to trust Him completely despite our fears, to experience inner peace during turmoil, or just praise God daily because He is worthy of our praise? Saying like Job, "Though He slay me yet will I trust Him?" or like Jacob, we hang on for dear life pleading, "I will not let Thee go unless you bless me?" Are we willing to pray, to praise, and to worship Him, even if for the moment, in His wisdom, He chooses not to bless us?

Bridgette has addressed the necessity and power of life saving prayer, not from a theoretical perspective, but from the vault of her own journey in the experiential knowledge and empirical encounter with transformative prayer. If there ever was a time, we needed such a testimony to the true nature and need of prayer, it is now.

This author has lifted the lid and raised the bar in both the invitation and the challenge to prayer by sharing her own triumphant battles in prayer. Prayer is not optional to our survival spiritually, it is essential. Bridgette invites us to continue this exciting and exhilarating journey with herself and many other payer-warriors as we pray, stand-still in prayer, and experience the life changing power of God's grace through prayer.

Ultimately, as we learn to walk with God through prayer in every way and in all circumstance of our lives, we will walk undefeated in this life and will one day walk with all prayer-warriors and with our Lord Himself into Glory. There our prayers will turn to praise, and praise to unalloyed worship of the One who answered our prayers, even before we asked, and while we were yet speaking. Let us join our friend and sister in Christ, Bridgette as we read these exciting prayer adventures in *Overcomer*.

Dr. Ernan A. Norman, M.Div., Dr. Min.
Pastor, Southern New England Conference SDA
Associate Professor of Theology & Religion – Atlantic Union College

Author's Preface

For several years, I have prayed for God to reveal my purpose in life. Over the past few years, He has made it clear that my purpose is to make it into heaven and to help others get there also. This book is written with that purpose in mind. It consists of selected personal and biblical stories of trials and triumphs that have been endured and achieved through prayer. Prayer is powerful. It changes people and circumstances. It has altered my perspective on life and allowed me to overcome dire situations that I never thought I could survive.

Being an overcomer, I have learned the importance of praying without ceasing. My love for God and others grows stronger when I pray frequently and persistently. Whenever I am spiritually weak and cannot pray, I know that there are others praying for me. Whenever a group commits to consistently pray, God moves mountains and manifests His power through miracles.

It is my sincere desire that you will get to know God personally and intimately through reading this book. For those of you who already know Him at this level, I encourage you to keep it up and go deeper. You will be inspired to pray sincerely and more often, whether in the midst of trials, or after being triumphant. For those who are still getting to know God, I recommend you spend quality time reading the Bible and talking to God as you would a friend.

To go deeper spiritually, we must be totally honest with ourselves and God. We must cry out to the Lord and seek Him with our whole heart. Without spiritual depth, we will tumble and crumble by any force. Without depth, we will be tossed and turned by the slightest wind. It is never enjoyable to be tossed around with no clear direction of a path forward. To attain the heights that God wants us to reach, we must go deeper. I want everyone reading this book to join me in going "deeper." I want you to join me in going deeper in the Lord, deeper in His Word, and deeper in prayer.

My prayer is that God will use this book to transform you. The conversion may manifest itself in different ways. For example, rather than complaining about a problem, you pray about it. Despite any fears, you trust Him completely. While in the midst of turmoil, you experience an inner peace. You will openly praise God on a daily basis, because He is worthy, and not only when He chooses to bless you.

I am not perfect, but I have gone through radical changes because of the power of prayer. That's why, I can boldly proclaim, *"I'm an Overcomer! Prayer Saved My Life!"* If you give it a chance, prayer will make a difference in your life too. God promised that "To him who overcomes I will grant to sit with Me on My throne, as I also overcame and sat down with My Father on His throne" (Revelation 3:21, NKJV). We can all be overcomers through prayer and God's saving grace.

Overcomer

Chapter 1: No Time To Pray

BAM!

Although it happened quickly, everything moved in slow motion. The trees outside the car were coming closer and closer. The car swayed, my body jerked forward, and my purse flew off the seat, seeking refuge on the floor.

> "Watch ye therefore, and pray always, that ye may be accounted worthy to escape all these things that shall come to pass, and to stand before the Son of man."
>
> (Luke 21:36, KJV)

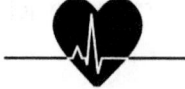

The smashing impact of the car against the guard rail deflated both air bags, resulting in pops reminiscent of gunshots. Within a twinkling of an eye, I had slammed into the guard rail and burst through it with my black 2000 Toyota Corolla. I was in a daze, and my eyes could not focus on anything.

In that moment before the impact, I did not have time to utter a word. I saw it coming, braced myself for the impact, but couldn't find any words to say within those split seconds. I did not have time to yell for anyone. I did not scream or shout for my mother, my husband, my daughters, or even my best friends.

Ironically, I always thought that in the moment of trouble, I would have enough time to call upon God. However, I did not get the chance to even whisper the name "JESUS." I never thought there might come a time when I needed Him, but could not open my mouth to call His name. Have you ever contemplated needing Jesus but not being able to call on Him?

This unforgettable moment of silence came for me one bright and sunny summer morning. It came with a BAM! It came when I was returning from an all-night prayer session at church. Throughout the night, we prayed for the church's spiritual revival as well as the physical and financial health of those we love.

During those hours of prayer and praise, it never crossed my mind that I might not live to see another day. I didn't worry about my husband and kids having to go on without me. During the service, I never once prayed for God to save my life. My prayer to live another day was unspoken, and right before the accident I did not have enough time to pray or to even call His name, but my God was right there.

I know God was with me because I broke free from the wreckage. As I climbed over the passenger side of my

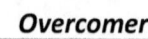
Overcomer

car and squeezed through the door, I was in total shock. My car was totaled, but there was not one scratch on my body. My Toyota Corolla was pulverized, but I was still in one piece.

The fender had crumbled, the engine was twisted, and the front of my car looked like a crushed soda can. The broken glass beneath my feet made crunching sounds as I slowly walked around the vehicle. The black tire marks on the highway told the scary tale of my brush with death. The dismantled guard rail shimmered in the sun and squeaked loudly as pieces hung off its base.

This same guard rail that I had burst through only a few minutes earlier was now cradling my car like a mother with her newborn baby. Before hitting the guard rail, I did not foresee the danger beyond those metal railings. A very steep hill and small rocky creek greeted me as I looked over the broken barrier. I then realized the extent of the danger God saved me from. Just then, I could not keep myself from praising Him.

I had to praise Him after surviving this horrific accident. I was standing next to the wreckage more grateful than I had been in years. I was standing as an overcomer because of my Savior. I was on the highway looking a mess with my clothing twisted and hair sticking up, but I was shouting praises to God. It was the kind of praise that elevates one to the presence of God.

I was singing words like "Thank you God for saving my life," "Oh, how sweet to trust in Jesus," and "Jesus loves me this I know." I know God heard my praises because a sense of calmness came over me despite being in a stressful situation. This calmness reassured me that God accepted my praise and worship. I felt that peace referred to in Philippians 4:7 (NJKV) which reminds us that "The peace of God, which surpasses all understanding, will guard your hearts and minds through Christ Jesus."

I should have been hyperventilating or at least weeping, but instead I was on a spiritual high on the side of the highway. I began telling the police officers and tow truck driver who came to help me about God and His love. As I held out my arms, touched my face and then my chest, I exclaimed, "Look, none of my bones are broken! God did this for me! He loves me and loves you too."

Sadly, I had previously missed many opportunities to share Jesus' love with others prior to my accident. If we are honest with ourselves, we have all missed those opportunities. Sometimes I did not proclaim my faith

Overcomer

because of fear, shame, and self-doubt. However, I knew after my accident that Jesus had saved my life for a reason. This realization helped me overcome my fright, embarrassment, and hesitancy to tell others about Jesus.

My accident became a real life testimony of God's amazing grace and love. I did not have any scratches, and initially, I did not feel any pain. I probably didn't feel it because of the adrenaline. However, when I got home, there was a sudden ache in my chest. Every time I felt that ache, I smiled from ear to ear. What a bittersweet pain! The sensational soreness was indeed a testimony of God's mercy.

Whenever my body ached, I hugged myself; and while embracing my chest, I reflected on the fact that the dead can feel no pain. So if I had died, I would not be experiencing any pain! He saved me, so I welcomed the discomfort and focused on God's many promises in the Bible. One of my favorites being, "Therefore, He is able to save completely those who come to God through Him, because He always lives to intercede for them" (Hebrews 7:25, NKJV).

Jesus is always praying for us even when we don't have the chance to pray. Jesus is our advocate at all times. This notion caused me to stop and re-evaluate my spiritual life and my relationship with God. I realized that God wanted me to go from a superficial high to spiritual depth. He wanted me to not only survive, but also to thrive as an overcomer.

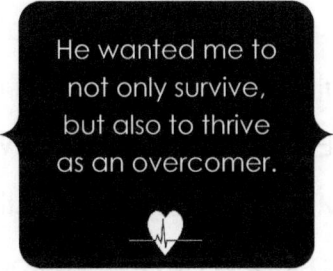
He wanted me to not only survive, but also to thrive as an overcomer.

This meant I needed to do more than simply attend church weekly and only study my Bible when it's convenient. I was to spend quality time with Him and live by His words each day. I had to go deeper spiritually where nothing and no one could shake my faith in Him. To attain this unshakeable faith, I needed to rely on Him completely like the legends did in biblical times.

Take for example, Moses, one of my favorite spiritual hall of famers. He went from a prince dwelling in a palace to being a murderer banished from Egypt. It must have been traumatic for Moses to go from a prince to a pauper. Shedding his Egyptian cover was undoubtedly an emotional and a spiritual low for Moses.

However, spending 40 years in the Midian desert allowed him to form a deeper relationship with God (Exodus 2:11-25, KJV). When he began to rely fully on God, Moses experienced intimacy with the Lord and was called "a friend of God" (Exodus 33:11, KJV). Moses was the only man allowed to climb Mount Sinai, be in the presence of God for 40 days, and live to tell about it.

A momentous life changing experience, like Moses had, is possible for us too. It starts with having a better prayer life and talking to God as you would a friend. Share everything in your heart, share often, and share in complete honesty. Share the good, the bad, and the ugly because whether our prayers are spoken or unspoken, there is power in prayer. This power will strengthen our spiritual muscles and resuscitate our spiritual lives. When we cannot shout or don't have enough time to audibly talk to God, it is reassuring to know that God answers unspoken prayers. Prayers uttered in our hearts years ago are still being answered today.

Prayers for our health, wealth, and well-being whispered in the prayer closets of our mothers, fathers, grandparents, and great-grandparents are now being manifested in our lives. Conversations we had with God and requests made in our prayer closets will come to fruition at the right time. Therefore, we should never miss an opportunity to pray.

My accident taught me that there will come a day when I won't have enough time to pray. That day will come for you too and it may be much sooner than you believe. This means we should maximize the time we have now. None of us should have to hit a guard rail on a busy highway in order to draw closer to God. We should proactively build an unbreakable bond with our Creator. This is possible - all we need to do is pray.

Lord, I know You're not subject to time. You exist in the past, present, and future. With You, "Lord one day is as a thousand years, and a thousand years as one day" (2 Peter 3:8, NKJV). This is reassuring to me because I am limited by time and more often than not, I don't spend my time wisely. I miss so many opportunities to pray and ask for protection as I go rushing through my days. In the future when I'm facing death or danger, but don't have enough time to call upon You, I want You to save me Lord. Save me because I'm not ready to die. Save me so I can testify of Your love and faithfulness. Save me, Lord!

Chapter 2: Don't Remove Prayer

What would make a grown man cry? I mean sob with such intensity that his tears are immortalized in scripture for eternity. The Bible says, "Peter remembered the word of Jesus, which said unto him, before the cock crow, thou shalt deny me thrice. And he went out, and wept bitterly" (Matthew 26:75, KJV). I was not there when the apostle Peter denied Christ, but I can feel his sorrow. How many times have we denied Christ to fit in with the crowd, to get a "great" job, or to propel our own selfish aspirations?

"Therefore to him that knoweth to do good, and doeth [it] not, to him it is sin."

(James 4:17, KJV)

For me, it was a typical day at work. I received an email that I was to be featured in an industry-leading magazine, spotlighting the "Who's Who" in Healthcare. I was elated about the possibility of seeing my name in the spotlight, or at least on printed pages, highlighting my accomplishments. It seemed to be a pretty simple process of answering a few questions via email and submitting a picture. While I was hesitant about the picture, I eagerly responded to the questions about my career progression, future aspirations, and what was important to me in life.

I recall writing several sentences about how I was a Christian and how prayer is the foundation of my spiritual life. The words flowed from my heart to my fingers, typing with eloquence and ease. I was able to submit the article within one hour and then dashed off to the next meeting.

Driving to another building for the upcoming meeting, the Holy Spirit asked me this question, "What would you do if you were asked to remove the reference to prayer from the article?" With arrogance and self-confidence, I thought to myself, *I would say, "No way." I am not removing the word "prayer" or any reference to it. I would withdraw my submission if I was asked to do such a thing.*

Doesn't this sound like the impetuous Peter who said "Lord, even though everyone deserts you, I would never desert you," (Matthew 26:33, KJV) but ended up denying Christ. I continued driving along the road with my pious indignation. I went through the rest of the day not realizing I had put the Holy Spirit in a corner. I had told Him I was in control and did not need any guidance. Self has a way of feeding our pride until we get so full that there is no room for God or anyone else.

Overcomer

Like any inflated balloon, pride will cause us to burst sooner or later. There is nothing more heart-wrenching than the sound of a popped balloon, especially at a party. Well, within three days, my balloon burst. One of the company's communication leaders reached out to me. He shared how excited he was about my responses and how he "hated to do this, but we would have to make some revisions."

One of the recommended revisions was to remove the word "prayer" from the article. I had mentioned "prayer" three times in the article and that was deemed three times too many by corporate standards. Without seeking any guidance from God, I agreed to remove two references to prayer and only leave one reference in the article. I didn't realize it then, but now I know that those three times were not random - one for the Father, one for the Son, and one for the Holy Spirit.

I did not think about it in that moment, but I had compromised my faith. Compromise is a poison. It's like a large cup of café mocha topped with whipped cream, cinnamon, and a swirl of chocolate, but spiked with arsenic. It will surely kill us, but the cup and contents look and taste so appealing that we happily embrace it, relishing every moment of the warm poison.

After denying my Lord and selling my soul for a quarter page in a magazine, I hung up the phone and continued working. A few hours later, the Holy Spirit reminded me of our conversation days earlier. At that moment, I understood a bit more why Peter wept bitterly. I felt like a traitor. I felt like the scum of the earth. My heart broke into pieces. I literally wanted to curl myself into a ball, crawl under my desk, and cry for days. To add insult to injury, the Holy Spirit initially tried to warn me that I would be placed in a compromising situation.

I was so full of self that I never stopped to ask the Holy Spirit, "Lord what should I do in that kind of situation?" "How may I use this opportunity to bring honor to your name?" All I had to do was ask, "Lord, what would you have me do?" I am confident the Lord would have given me the answer and I would not have failed that test.

For those of you who are in school, or remember your time in school, you know that there are always tests. To get to the next level in each class, you have to pass various tests. It is no different in our spiritual lives. We must take and pass tests each and every day. I was so focused on being noted as a "Who's Who" that I forgot whose I was and whom I served.

> I failed this test because I thought I could overcome on my own.

I failed this test because I thought I could overcome on my own. I did not seek guidance or heed the warnings of the Holy Spirit. Now every student knows that if they failed, their last hope is to ask the teacher for a retake. The only thing I could do in my situation was pray that the Master Teacher would allow me to retake the test.

Nearly eight months after this ordeal, God answered my prayers and granted me a re-test! The Bible reminds us, "Oh, give thanks to the LORD, for *He is* good! For His mercy *endures* forever" (Psalms 136:1, KJV). I had the opportunity to be spotlighted again. However, this article was to be published through the company's intranet site for all employees. The article focused on the "mind, body, spirit" philosophy. I was asked to share how I lead my team as well as remain stress-free and focused during a hectic day at work. I decided to focus on how prayer helps me throughout my day.

After submitting the article, the editor sent me a proof in which the references to prayer were removed from the article. I prayed immediately and asked God for guidance. I had two options: accept the revised version, or ask that my original content be put back in the article. With the Holy Spirit's guidance, I was able to recognize that this was the same test from eight months earlier. I made the conscious decision not to compromise or reject my Lord this time around. We never have to compromise when given the option to deny our faith.

I sent an email to the editor saying, "I have added the spiritual content back in the article. It is essential to who I am, so I do not want it omitted. If it cannot be included for corporate reasons, I understand, but I will have to pull my submission." Her response was simply, "Thanks. I think we will be fine." Not only was it nice to be featured on the company's website, but what brought me true joy was knowing that God had forgiven me. He allowed me to retake the test and He guided me throughout the entire process because I prayed to Him and asked for guidance. I overcame because of God's guidance.

Overcomer

After Peter denied Christ three times, Jesus gave him a chance to redeem himself. He asked Peter three times, "Simon, son of Jonah, do you love Me?" (John 21:15-18, NKJV). Christ wanted to restore Peter and make sure that he was fully prepared to continue His ministry. Throughout our day, we are faced with situations that may require us to figuratively remove the word prayer or compromise our faith. Jesus is doing everything to prepare us for these situations and to restore us fully if we miss the mark. Knowing that Christ's will is to restore us into a perfect relationship with Him, it is important that we never compromise.

Compromising weakens us spiritually and pulls us away from God. Whether it's removing the word "prayer" from the article, cutting corners on a lucrative business deal, or succumbing to worldly pleasures, the result is the same – spiritual death. We will never overcome if we compromise. Staying connected to God is the only path that leads to life. This connection is the only way we can ensure we do not compromise and we are prepared for life's upcoming tests. Are you ready for your test?

God, I know a test is coming soon. Teach me how to prepare for the trials I will encounter in

life. Holy Spirit, alert me before I am in a compromising situation. When tested, I no longer want to make concessions to fit in. I don't want to deny You in order to be recognized by others. My desire is to be ready and make You proud of me. Jesus, I know You're doing everything You can to prepare me for my tests. I am grateful.

Chapter 3: Underwater Prayer

I remember gasping for air and floundering underwater during one of the scariest moments of my young life. I was about seven years old when I almost drowned in my school's pool. I was not a

> *"But when he saw that the wind was boisterous, he was afraid; and beginning to sink he cried out, saying, "Lord, save me!"*
>
> (Matthew 14:30, NKJV)

mischievous kid who decided to swim without supervision. On the contrary, I was in a swimming class and instructed to swim several laps in the pool.

I had done a few laps when my legs began to cramp, fear took hold of me, and I immediately started sinking to the bottom of the pool. Prayer did not enter my mind. Instead, I frantically threw my arms and legs around trying to get back to the surface. Out of nowhere, I felt someone pulling on my shoulders and bathing suit. I began pushing, kicking and fighting in hysteria, not realizing this person was trying to help me. I was released from their grasp during the tussle and instantaneously began to sink again.

Bridgette Bastien

As I sank below the seven feet pool marker, I was sure death would overtake me. I was mentally preparing for my watery grave when the strong arm of my swim coach grabbed me from behind. He then masterfully pulled me to the pool's edge. I remember laying on the cold concrete crying and staring up at the blue skies painted with white fluffy clouds. Those clouds brought me some comfort that traumatic day.

About 25 years after my initial brush with death, I had another underwater experience which is also etched in my memory. No one could tell I was shedding tears in this case. My husband, a friend, and I were snorkeling in the Indian Ocean while vacationing in the Maldives. As I explored the ocean floor, I was in awe of this underwater world. The clear, blue scenery, swaying effervescent seaweed, baby sharks, schools of fish, and picturesque coral took my breath away.

Everything was moving or swaying rhythmically when I saw the most magnificent sea turtle, weighing hundreds of pounds. The turtle dived several feet underwater, then effortlessly ascended to catch its breath. Its movements were like a well-choreographed artistic dance beneath the ocean's surface. As I watched nature displaying its power, grace, and agility, tears trickled from my eyes and onto my goggles.

Although I was crying, I was not that scared seven-year-old. I felt very secure underwater in this peaceful and mesmerizing aqua world. The joy in my heart and the scenery were confirmation that God exists and that He is, indeed, the Creator. I uttered a brief prayer of thanksgiving while diving deeper towards the ocean floor and mimicking the turtle's movements. I said in my heart, "Thank you God for your creativity and divine wisdom. Indeed, everything you have made is perfect. This beauty I am seeing now, beneath this ocean, leaves me in awe."

The underwater scenery was truly a sight to behold, so now whenever I feel life pulling me down and my problems become unbearable, I close my eyes and remember being underwater. I reflect on the day I spent snorkeling in the Indian Ocean instead of those frightening moments in the pool. I reminisce about my prayer of thanksgiving. I recall how the magnificent sea turtle never struggled or fought to breathe like I did as a child. Instead, the turtle ascended to the top of the water and exhaled with a sense of purpose.

The sea creature knew instinctively that exhaling was the body's natural way of releasing tension. Overcomers know that praying is the supernatural way to get a spiritual breakthrough.

> Overcomers know that praying is the supernatural way to get a spiritual breakthrough.

Prayer helps us deal with life whether we are above or beneath water. Do you feel as if life is pushing you underwater? What is your reaction when underwater or when faced with difficult situations in life?

Our reaction, when underwater, is a good indication of our relationship with Christ and the health of our prayer lives. If our first reaction is to pray, it shows that we put our trust in God. If our natural tendency is to fight others or frantically try to save ourselves, we may need to re-evaluate our faith in God. When life has us underwater, we can only overcome through prayer.

This was clearly understood by the disciple Peter during his underwater experience on the Sea of Galilee. Matthew 14:20-33 KJV recaps the story of Jesus feeding the multitude and then making the disciples get into a boat to go to the other side of the sea. Shortly afterwards, the boat was tossed by a furious storm and the disciples became crippled with fear. Peter then saw Jesus walking on water and boldly asked Jesus if he could join Him. Peter, a mere man, walked on water, that is, until he took his eyes off Jesus.

Within moments of looking away, Peter began sinking beneath the stormy waves. Peter instinctively did what we should do when overpowered by the storms of life. He cried out "Lord, save me." These are some of most beautiful words ever uttered in conversation with Jesus. Peter's prayer was not long winded, it was simple and impactful. When we're underwater, we don't have to be eloquent. Underwater prayers require honesty, submission and repentance. Such prayers allow us to let go of everything that is unimportant and grab onto God. It's reassuring to know that sincere prayers always transcend this earth and reach the throne room of God.

Jesus' response to Peter's prayer was immediate, as He stretched out His hand and grab a hold of Peter. To get above water, all we need to do is cry out with our arms stretched towards our Savior. Jesus answered his prayer right away and revealed the battle within Peter's heart. "O you of little faith," He said, "Why did you doubt?" (Matthew 14:31, NKJV). Doubt and fear are always present when we are underwater because we tend to focus on the chaos around us.

Instead of focusing on the strong winds and heavy rain that come with the storms of life, I am learning to keep my eyes on God. Revelations 15:2 (KJV) says "And I saw as it were a sea of glass mingled with fire: and them that had gotten the victory over the beast, and over his image, and over his mark, and over the number of his name, stand on the sea of glass, having the harps of God." We will not only overcome and be victorious, but also stand on the sea of glass in heaven if we make God our primary focus.

Through prayer and relying completely on God, we will indeed walk on water. Praying is the best option to survive and be victorious, whether our underwater experience is that of almost drowning in a pool or snorkeling in a beautiful ocean. Jesus showed by His interaction with Peter, that when we hold onto God, there is no other direction to go, but upwards. Prayer is indeed the ultimate life saver.

Jesus, You know the ups and downs of life. You faced storms when You were on earth and You walked on water. Teach me not to flounder when underwater. Help me to rely on prayer and

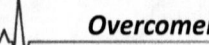 *Overcomer*

reach for Your strong arms that are always out-stretched in my direction. The next time life tries to drown me, I will cry out to You, "Lord, save me!"

Chapter 4: United Prayer

The dark days went on for many, many months. This was the period in my life when I had no desire or interest in anything spiritual. I struggled in different areas of my life because I was not communing with God. I would actually go several days without real prayer.

> *"These all continued with one accord in prayer and supplication."*
>
> *(Acts 1:14, KJV)*

I would do the quick prayer before meals, before I drove out of my garage, or before bed. However, there was no intimacy with God. I would attempt to read, but would wake up several minutes later with my face in the Bible. I would have no recollection of the words I had just read. During these dark days, something inside of me kept crying out – "God, please help!"

A church sister called one day during these dark months and asked me to join the prayer line. She told me, "The prayer line is a phone conference involving a group of like-minded individuals sharing their prayer requests and interceding for each other." I hesitantly called the number because I did not know who would be on the phone or what to expect.

The leader of the prayer group was very excited to hear my voice and welcomed me over and over again. She shared with the group that God had been telling her to reach out to me. As she shared how God had been urging her to connect with me, I smiled from ear to ear. Her story was another confirmation that God truly loves me. He had heard my cry for help and already had a plan in place to answer my prayers.

For the next five years, these prayer warriors and I lifted our petitions to God on a daily basis and spiritually we grew stronger. This group still meets regularly to pray and discuss the Bible. We share our experiences, ask questions, and support each other. The best part of being a member is that we PRAY. We fast and pray for our church, our families, those in need (spiritually, financially, physically), world leaders, various crises and disasters, and for each other. I witnessed first-hand the manifestation and power of prayer.

Through this group, we have had so many prayers answered, including physical and spiritual healings, job promotions, opportunities for employment, academic breakthroughs, etc. I vividly remember one of our church sisters being diagnosed with cancer and given only a few months to live. Her doctors had given up hope and recommended that she put her house in order and prepare to die.

Although the doctors gave up, we did not. We started to earnestly pray for her. Even when she lost her hair, the palm of her hands turned slightly black, and the burning sensation of her skin got worse, we did not stop praying. After months of fasting and praying together, her cancer went into remission and she is still alive today. Some may say her remission is the result of an aggressive treatment. I believed my church sister overcame cancer and received her breakthrough as a result of united prayer.

She triumphed over this terrible disease because her friends and family kept the faith and interceded for her daily. Today, she wears her pink pin in pride and prays for other women fighting their own breast cancer battles. She not only survived a horrific life event and is thriving, but also dedicates her time, talent, and treasures in support of other women. Like a true overcomer, her life's mission is now helping others defeat the unbeatable.

Overcomer

Witnessing this breakthrough, I often wonder why our entire church is not the prayer group. This is not an elitist club or secret society

> Like a true overcomer, her life's mission is now helping others defeat the unbeatable.

in which only a few church members can participate. This is an open group, and we have regularly asked the church body to be a part of it. Some members have openly refused, while others promise to join, but do not follow through. We continue to pray that they will eventually join the prayer group. Nevertheless, the group remains intact with a faithful few. We remain united in prayer and come to God in one accord.

The Bible is clear that there are benefits of united prayer. "If two of you shall agree on earth as touching anything that they shall ask, it shall be done for them of my Father which is in heaven. For where two or three are gathered together in my name, there am I in the midst of them" (Matthew 18:19-20, KJV). We miss out on so many blessings because we are not united in Christ. We will happily rearrange our schedule and come together for a party, cookout, or a football game, but we hesitate when we have to come together for prayer. Do you hesitate to pray with others?

It is often said, "Much prayer, much power." The power of prayer was evident in Acts 1:12-14 (KJV). The disciples, among a group of 120 people, prayed in an upper room after Christ's death. There was unity among the disciples. Their prayer was so pure and powerful that the Holy Spirit descended upon them with the sound of a great wind and with tongues of fire. They began to speak in other languages and to preach boldly in the name of Christ, which resulted in 3,000 converts to Christianity. United prayer requires being in one accord. United prayer always results in power and manifestation of the Holy Spirit.

This power was not just for the disciples of old. There is power for us today when we pray as a family unit, together with friends, church members, and even with strangers. When we unite and pray together, Christ is with us and the Holy Spirit brings our prayers to heaven's throne room in a manner pleasing to God. When we pray together, there is an earthly and heavenly unity. We often do not experience this oneness in Christ because we refuse to pray together.

Furthermore, there are often distractions when we attempt to talk to our Heavenly Father. Do you notice during your family worship time that someone is always acting up and refusing to pray or participate? Do you notice at church that whenever it is time to pray, someone is being irreverent by walking in the sanctuary or cell phones start ringing? This is not by accident, but rather a plot by the devil to hinder our united prayer and weaken our spiritual power.

"United we stand and divided we fall" is a common saying and a reality in our spiritual life. Christ asked His disciples to watch and pray with Him in the Garden of Gethsemane, but instead, they fell asleep. They missed a once in a lifetime chance to intervene for Jesus in His moment of need. They missed out because they were sleeping instead of praying. Why are we collectively sleeping?

Most of the time we hesitate to participate in united prayer; but by doing so, we lose out on so many blessings. The fear of being vulnerable, praying out loud, or joining a new group should never outweigh the benefits of spending time with God. God's will for our families and churches is that we come together as one unified body.

United prayer gives us power - power to reflect Christ in any situation, power to praise in the midst of painful circumstances, and power to pull others out of their dark days and help heal their brokenness. Praying together and praying for each other are the missing links in our prayer chain. It is not enough to pray by ourselves. We are called to pray in unity with others.

Jesus, I know it's a privilege to pray. Remind me of that fact, whenever I get a chance to pray with and for others. I may not always be comfortable speaking to You or sharing in an open forum, but it's not about my comfort level. You told us in Your Word to come together and bring our requests to Your throne room. I want to be obedient and join with my friends and family in prayer on a consistent basis.

Overcomer

Chapter 5: Teacup Prayer

I could barely breathe and pain raced through my body. It felt as if someone was jumping up and down on my heart and lungs in concrete spiked shoes. I listened on the prayer line as my sisters and brothers in Christ discussed the Word of God and rejoiced in His glory.

> *"Therefore, because the king's command was urgent, and the furnace exceedingly hot, the flame of the fire killed those men who took up Shadrach, Meshach, and Abed-Nego."*
>
> *(Daniel 3:22, KJV)*

After discussing various Scriptures, it was time for prayer. I did not feel like praying, but I have learned that whenever I do not feel like praying, I should pray. I offered to pray. As I opened my mouth, the sadness in my heart poured out over the phone line. After the prayer conference call ended, I stood in my kitchen for several minutes trying to garner enough strength to take the next steps and get ready for the day.

I did not want to go to work. I only wanted to curl up in bed and sleep the day away. My job had become so stressful, the team so despondent, and the environment so cut-throat and toxic that I wanted to be anywhere else but work. For the past several months, I had been working longer hours, spending less and less time with my family, and missing out on special moments with my children. I felt like I was in quicksand grasping at branches and struggling to make it out alive.

The phone ringing pulled me from my trance and day-mare about work. I answered the phone, and almost immediately, I recognized the voice on the other end of the line. It was a member of our prayer group. I barely said hello when my church sister said, "I could hear the sadness in your voice as you prayed this morning. I had to call you before you left for work."

Tears started flowing from my eyes and the only words I could say were, "Thank you." My heart was filled with both appreciation and sadness. She then said, "Before I pray, do you mind if I share this story with you? The story is about a teacup. It is by an unknown author and it goes like this:"

> There was a couple who used to go to England to shop. They both liked antiques and pottery (especially teacups). This was their twenty-fifth wedding

anniversary so they decided to go shopping. In this quaint shop, they saw a beautiful teacup set sitting on a velvet cloth on the top shelf. They said to the shopkeeper, "May we see that? We've never seen one quite so beautiful." As the lady handed it to them, suddenly the teacup spoke. "You don't understand," it said. "I haven't always been a teacup. There was a time when I was a lump of red clay. My master took me, rolled me and patted me over and over until I yelled out, "Let me alone," but he only smiled and said, "Not yet."

"I was placed on a spinning wheel," the cup said, "and suddenly I was spun around and around and around. Stop it! I'm getting dizzy!" I screamed. But the master only nodded and said, "Not yet." He then put me in the oven. I never felt such heat! I wondered why he wanted to burn me, and I yelled and knocked at the door. I could see him through the opening and I could read his lips as He shook his head and said, "Not yet."

Finally, the door opened, he put me on the shelf, and I began to cool down. "There, that's better," I said. And he brushed and painted me all over. The fumes were horrible. I thought I would gag. "Stop it, stop it!" I cried. He only nodded, "Not yet." Then suddenly he put me back into the oven, not like the first one. This was twice as hot and I knew I would suffocate. I begged. I pleaded. I screamed. I cried. All the time I could see him through the opening, nodding his head saying, "Not yet." Then I knew there wasn't any hope. I would never make it. I was ready to give up. But the door opened and he took me out and placed me on the shelf. One hour later he handed me a mirror and said, "Look at yourself." And I did. I said, "That's not me; that couldn't be me. It's beautiful. I'm beautiful."

"I want you to remember," he said, "I know it hurts to be rolled and patted, but if I had left you alone, you'd have dried up. I know it made you dizzy to spin you around on the wheel, but if I had stopped, you would have crumbled. I knew it hurt and was hot in the oven, but if I hadn't put you there, you would have cracked. I know the fumes were bad when I brushed and painted you all over, but if I hadn't done that, you never would have hardened; you would not have had any color in your life. And if I hadn't put you back in that second oven, you wouldn't survive for very long because the hardness would not have held. Now you are a finished product. You are what I had in mind when I first saw you as that red clay.'"

I was so overwhelmed by the story that I could not speak. I simply knelt on the floor in silence as my church sister prayed for me. She thanked God for creating me and for using me to bless others. She praised God for keeping me sane despite my chaotic job. She asked God

Overcomer

to remind me that everything I go through is for a purpose. She predicted that I would be an overcomer by the grace of God and that I would be like that beautiful teacup on a velvet cloth on the top shelf.

Her prayer touched the depth of my soul and erased the fears, doubts, and sadness I was experiencing in that moment. She strengthened me and lifted my spirit with her sincere teacup prayer. A teacup prayer is one in which we pray for someone else in their moment of weakness. A teacup prayer is one in which God uses us to speak hope to those who are downhearted, peace to those in tempestuous situations and life to those contemplating death.

As I listened to her pray, I kept thinking about how I am, indeed, a teacup. I had been rolled, spilled, heated, polished, and re-heated over the past three years. Just when life seemed too calm, something else would happen and I would go spiraling into despair and desperation again. Like this teacup, when Christ was molding and fashioning me in His image, I cried, "Why me Lord?" I pleaded with Him, "No more pain and drama." I screamed, "Jesus, please stop it!"

During my seasons of outcry, God remained silent or He simply replied, "Not yet!" It is difficult to wait when all you want is closure. It is difficult to keep a positive attitude while on a spinning wheel. It is difficult to pray when in the oven of spiritual refinement. This is why my church sister's prayer was so powerful. She spoke directly to my heart.

While my church sister prayed for me, I could feel the weight of sadness being lifted off my shoulders. I could feel the shackles of doubt being removed from my feet. I could feel the hardness of my heart being softened by the reassurance of God's love. God used her to shine a light in the darkness of my soul.

Her teacup prayer opened the flood gates and I began sobbing. A teacup prayer can turn our private sessions of crying into corporate praise. She said with love, "God is going to make you so beautiful. He is going to elevate you to heights you have never dreamed about. Although you do not see it now and do not understand, trust Him and know that He is making you into a masterpiece for His glory." She reinforced what God had been telling me for several months: First, the heated crucible was not meant to destroy me, but to make me stronger. Second, I would be so strengthened by my experience that nothing would be able to shake my faith. Third, I will help change lives by freely sharing my testimony - the testimony of an overcomer who goes through many trials, but continues to rise up in God's strength and reflect His character.

> The testimony of an overcomer who goes through many trials, but continues to rise up in God's strength and reflect His character.

I truly want to reflect Christ like the three Hebrew boys - Meshach, Shadrach and Abednego - in the Bible. These young men always walked, talked, looked and acted like Christ even when thrown into a fiery furnace. Being Christ-like ensures that I would not smell like smoke and my clothes would not be scorched even after being in fire. Instead of becoming unrecognizable, like something burnt to ashes, God would "give me beauty for ashes, oil of joy for mourning and garment of praise for spirit of heaviness" (Isaiah 61:3, NKJV). I would be re-created in a new image because of God's grace and the many teacup prayers offered for me.

Have you ever experienced a teacup prayer? There are many examples in the Bible - my favorite is in Acts 12

(NKJV). The apostle Peter was imprisoned by King Herod because he belonged to the church. Peter's church family earnestly prayed for him and God moved in a powerful way. God's response was immediate and miraculous. The Bible says, "When she, [Rhoda – the servant girl], recognized Peter's voice, because of her gladness she did not open the gate, but ran in and announced that Peter stood before the gate. But they said to her, "You are beside yourself!" Yet she kept insisting that it was so. So they said, "It is his angel" (Acts 12:14-15, NKJV).

God sent an angel to rescue Peter from prison while his church family was praying a teacup prayer for him. They prayed for Peter in his weakest moment. Peter arrived at Mary's house after his prison break, but his church family was in disbelief when they saw him. The church's prayers broke the chains from his wrists and feet. Teacup prayers set us free, strengthen our faith, turn our crying into praise and worship, and reveal God's love – a love that never fails.

We have all been teacups at some point. A teacup, no matter how beautiful it looks on the outside, is fragile. For a teacup to endure the refining process, it needs divine intervention and intercessory prayers. Prayers prevent us from cracking or being completely shattered when others use us for their own enjoyment. It's those prayers that allow us to overcome the spinning, rolling, patting, painting, and heating that we all have to go through in the furnace of life.

    I am a teacup - I have been in life's oven, terrified that I would be overcome by the heat. I am a teacup - I have been on the top shelf being admired because of my divinely decorated life. I am a teacup - I know my external beauty is not diminished when I am placed next to another divinely designed teacup. I am a teacup - I reflect the image of my Maker and I bring delight to all those who behold me. I am a teacup – I, too, have to offer teacup prayers for others.

Lord, I come to You on behalf of other teacups. Like I did, they may see themselves as solely pieces of clay. They might feel that there is nothing special about them. Help them to see Your image in their reflections. Allow them to recognize that being rolled, patted, kneaded, and heated is not meant to break them, but to make them stronger and more beautiful. Elevate them to the top so they can shine and You can be glorified.

Chapter 6: Punk Rock Prayer

Have you ever been stranded and needed someone's help? My husband and I were recently reminiscing about our highway adventure. We drove from Connecticut to Massachusetts on a cold wintery day. The journey was uneventful until we arrived in Worcester, Massachusetts.

> "Which of these three do you think was a neighbor to the man who fell into the hands of robbers? The expert in the law replied "The one who had mercy on him. Jesus told him, 'Go and do likewise.' "
>
> (Luke 10:36-37, KJV)

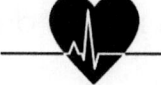

Out of nowhere, our SUV started clanging, sputtering, rattling, and then abruptly stopped in the middle of the busy highway. Just imagine, being stuck with a one-year-old baby during the winter in a stalled SUV amidst speeding vehicles. We thought for sure that one of the speeding cars or trucks would hit our SUV and thrust us over the embankment or into the snow pile hills along the highway.

We immediately put on the hazard signal, then my husband went outside in the freezing weather to get help. With the SUV not running, it was not long before it became extremely cold inside the vehicle. I bundled up my baby girl the best I could and watched as my husband frantically tried to wave down passing cars.

No one attempted to help us for over 30 minutes. We saw business men and women drive by without blinking an eye. We saw minivans pass by filled with happy parents and children. We saw countless individuals change lanes and keep their heads straight. There was not one highway patrol officer in sight and no one cared enough to stop and help us. Would you have stopped to help us?

My husband shivered outside and our daughter started crying inside the vehicle from being cold. I began doubting that anyone would assist us. I silently prayed, "Lord, please send someone to help us. We are in danger with cars and trucks flying by constantly and the temperature dropping." After praying, I felt reassured that someone would rescue us. I started looking through the back window in anticipation.

It was less than 5 minutes later that a couple, wearing all black, pulled up and stopped to help us. The guy had on black pants and a thick leather jacket with a punk rock band t-shirt peeking through it. He jumped out of his truck, and approached my husband with a concerned look on his face. They talked for a while, then my husband came back to our vehicle. With relief in his voice, he said, "They will give us a jump."

After our SUV started, the couple offered to drive behind us for a while to ensure we were safe. Once we got to a safe location and our vehicle was warm again, they wished us well and drove off. Though my husband offered, they refused to be compensated for their generosity. My heart was touched by these Good Samaritans.

Most churchgoers know the story of the Good Samaritan in the Bible. The Bible records, "A certain man went down from Jerusalem to Jericho, and fell among thieves, which stripped him of his raiment, and wounded him, and departed, leaving him half dead" (Luke 10:30, KJV). While this man was in distress, he waited for help just like my family did on that snow-covered busy highway. Several people passed him by without a thought of attending to his needs.

The Bible says a priest and a Levite saw this man bleeding and simply crossed to the other side of the road. Jesus revealed the lack of compassion of these law abiding church leaders who did not want to become religiously unclean by touching the bleeding man. They may have been highly regarded in the temple, but they were being chastised by the God of the temple. I have always wondered how many Bible carrying Christians saw us destitute and cold on that day, but changed lanes anyway.

The story continues, "But a certain Samaritan, as he journeyed, came where he was: and when he saw him, he had compassion on him" (Luke 10:33, KJV). This Samaritan saw the same scenery as the priest and Levite. He saw the man's bruises, saw his face covered in blood, saw his clothes torn, and heard him whimpering in pain. However, he did not look away because he had sympathy for the injured man.

The punk rock couple saw our stranded vehicle and my husband shivering in his snow-covered jacket, and they had compassion. They had a choice to make as they saw us on the side of that road. They could have changed lanes, or like the other drivers, turned a blind eye. However, their empathy propelled them into action and they became our lifeline.

The Good Samaritan not only cleaned the man up, put him on his horse, and brought him to someone who could care for his wounds, but also offered to cover the cost. The punk rock couple not only gave us a jump, but also drove behind us until we got to a safe location. By societal norms, the Samaritan should not have stopped to help because he was regarded as second-class citizen by Jewish standards. I would never have imagined that a punk rock couple would have stopped to help us. Both the Samaritan and this couple went above and beyond because of the love of Jesus in them.

Jesus told the Good Samaritan's story in response to a lawyer asking Him, "Who is my neighbor?" The question was meant to trick Jesus, but His response showed that being a neighbor is about love - the kind of love that propels us to meet the needs of others, even if it means inconveniencing ourselves or sacrificing for complete strangers.

The need in this world is great, but each day we tend to look the other way. We often fail the test of compassion because of prejudices, self-interest, busy life, etc. We fail the empathy test because we do not pray for others like Jesus prayed while He was on earth. We pray for ourselves and our selfish needs, while all around us are people crying out for help.

> No matter what season of life we are in, we will not overcome without prayer.

We ignore the cry of those in need because we get accustomed to it, it gets drowned out in the sea of other raging sounds, or we truly do not care about the suffering of others. The sad reality of the latter point is that life is cyclical and each of us, at some time or another, will cry out for help. When we are on the mountain top, it is difficult to fathom ever needing help from anyone, but when we descend or fall from the mountain, we quickly realize that we need someone else to pull us up.

We need each other whether we are on the mountain top looking down or in the valley trying to climb to its zenith. The highs and lows of life are seasonal and cyclical. No matter what season of life we are in, we will not overcome without prayer. Prayer is practical, powerful and transformational. Therefore, we should pray before becoming stranded on the highways of life. We ought to pray to be like the Good Samaritan and the punk rock couple. We need to pray to be a blessing to others while they are in their crisis.

God expects us to pray for power then go out into the world impacting and influencing lives for His glory. This is what the young captive girl from Israel did for Naaman and his wife (2 Kings 5, KJV). Her job was to serve his wife, but she had sympathy for Naaman when she saw him suffering from leprosy. Naaman was the commander of the king of Aram's army and was a highly regarded man. However, his power and stature in society could not heal his disease.

I can imagine the young slave girl praying for God to help Naaman. Although she was enslaved, she knew who she was and that she belonged to God. The Bible says, "For whatever is born of God overcomes the world. And this is the victory that has overcome the world - our faith" (1 John 5:4, NKJV). Her prayer enabled her to speak these words in faith to her mistress, "If only my master would see the prophet who is in Samaria! He would cure him of his leprosy" (2 Kings 5:3, KJV). She was risking her job, and potentially her life, by making such an unbelievable recommendation.

If Naaman had not been healed after seeing Elisha, the name of God would have been ridiculed and this young girl would have been in serious trouble. Her compassion to pray for someone who was enslaving her,

Overcomer

coupled with her faith to boldly proclaim that Naaman would be healed, made a difference. Naaman overcame his disease, which isolated him from society, because he believed the young girl and obeyed the servant of God.

These examples are for us. We need to proactively pray to help others regardless of how they treat us or what authority they may have over us. There are opportunities each day for us to bless others. In Ephesians 2:10 (KJV), the Bible reminds us that God not only enables us to do good works, but He has also prepared them in advance for us to do! We are already equipped with what is necessary to make a difference in someone's life.

How often do we pray that we are in the right place at the right time to help someone in need? We pray for help, but we need to pray to be the helper. We have to become more purposeful in praying to meet the needs of others. Such a prayer should not be viewed as something extraordinary. It should be our daily prayer and daily purpose to look for those in need and make a difference in their lives. We are called to be Good Samaritans and punk rock helpers.

Open my eyes, Jesus, as I go through my day so I can see those who are down-and-out. Sometimes, I am sensitive to the needy and I assist in whatever ways I can. Other times, I am so focused on my own issues that I overlook those who are crying out for help. I want to have a spirit of love and servitude so I don't look away from or step over anyone who needs a helping hand or is in danger. Give me a Good Samaritan's heart.

Chapter 7: Red Dress Prayer

Challenges in life make us bitter or make us better. With this thought in mind, I asked my prayer group to go out of their way to be a blessing to someone, not including their family and friends. The group was open

"But to do good and to communicate forget not: for with such sacrifices God is well pleased."

(Hebrews 13:16, KJV)

to the test because we had been through so much together.

Our prayer family meets three times a day over the phone to pray, study scripture, and encourage each other. For the past year and a half, our experiences together have renewed our spiritual walks, strengthened our characters, and stimulated our desires to seek and serve God. It is with the desire to seek and serve God that they agreed to my challenge and eagerly shared their testimonies the following day.

The testimonies, of buying lunch for colleagues at work, giving food to the homeless on the highway, and helping a neighbor in need, were so inspirational that I extended the challenge for another week. I prayed earnestly that night and asked God to use me to be a blessing. I had no clue how quickly that prayer would be answered or that it would require self-sacrifice.

The next day we were in church having an annual celebration filled with praise and worship. A member of the church knelt next to me and whispered, "What you are wearing is so beautiful. Is it a skirt?" "No, it is actually a dress," I replied. She then said, "Aww, your red dress is beautiful, but I wish it was a skirt." This comment intrigued me, so I asked, "Why?" She explained that her daughter needed a red skirt to perform in a praise dance. Without a second thought, I said, "You can have my red dress."

She looked at me puzzled and asked, "What are you going to be wearing while she is performing?" At that moment, I recalled that I had a change of clothes in the car. I quietly left the sanctuary, retrieved my jeans and sweater from the car, and quickly changed out of my red dress. I handed my red dress over to the young lady and then returned to the sanctuary. I sat back down in the pew and continued praising and worshipping God. That simple act of kindness taught me more than I ever imagined throughout the course of the day.

Over the next few hours, several people questioned why I had changed out of my red dress and why I was wearing jeans. Some folks were curious because I had changed during the service. Others were questioning why I would be in church on the Sabbath, during the divine hour, in jeans. For the most part, I smiled and gave general answers to the various questions. I had no intention of having the young lady feel uncomfortable about needing my dress. I had no intention of feeding the unchristian-like curiosity. I had no intention of belittling the answer to my red dress prayer.

My prayer to bless someone was answered that day. My prayer to bless someone gave me a glimpse into what Christ did for me. Like Christ in His heavenly glory, my red dress covered me. I was beautifully adorned when I first walked into church. However, someone needed my covering so they, too, could give glory to God. Just as Christ removed His divinity and put on humanity to come to this earth, I removed my red dress and put on jeans to bless someone else. As Christ in His humanity was ridiculed, despised, and rejected of man, I was questioned repeatedly about changing into jeans.

As Christ's sacrifice ensured salvation to all who believe, my red dress sacrifice put a smile on the face of a young lady. Being a blessing to someone requires a sacrifice. We often

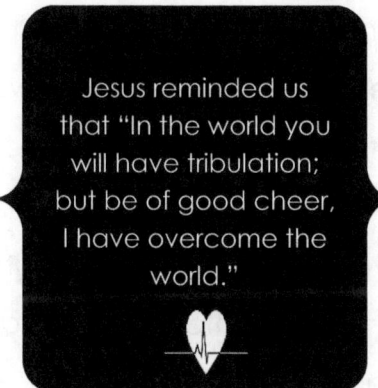

give out of our abundance, but true giving requires that we give all with a cheerful heart. Sacrifice strips us of our worldly power, possessions, and pride. Sacrifice sometimes means enduring tribulation and being ridiculed by others. Christ experienced this first hand, but did not hesitate to go all the way to Calvary.

Jesus reminded us that "In the world you will have tribulation; but be of good cheer, I have overcome the world" (John 16:33, NKJV). He highlighted being an overcomer of the world to emphasize the benefits of sacrificing for others. When we give all that we have, we become filled with heavenly love. When we give all that we have, we become rich. When we give all that we have, we please God.

God is well pleased whenever we bless others and reflect the love of Christ. God was pleased with my red dress prayer. God will be pleased with your red dress or red tie prayer. There is always someone in need and we often have the resources to meet that need. Sometimes we're not equipped to sacrifice. Before we leave home, we need to put on the right attire. We need to be clothed with the righteousness and love of Christ in order to make sacrifices.

As a mother, I have learned the true meaning of sacrifice. Sacrifice means giving up everything out of love for the sake of someone else. It's forgetting you are sick as you stay up all night while your child coughs, throws up, or whimpers in your arms. It means working several jobs or long hours so your children or siblings can have a better education and brighter future. It's hearing your stomach growl and gurgle from hunger, but going without food so your children can have enough to eat.

Many mothers have sacrificed their needs and aspirations for the well-being of their family. One notable mother that exemplified sacrifice was the widow of Zarephath. She sacrificed her last meal for a complete stranger at the risk of her son's life. 1 Kings 17:10-13 (KJV) recaps how Elijah asked this widow for some bread and she replied, "As the LORD thy God liveth, I have not a cake, but an handful of meal in a barrel, and a little oil in a cruse: and, behold, I am gathering two sticks, that I may go in and dress it for me and my son, that we may eat it, and die." Elijah then requested that she first make a small loaf of bread for him.

The widow of Zarephath gave her red dress that day because she did what Elijah said without hesitation. She made the bread for him with her last jar of flour and oil. I can imagine her praying while she kneaded the flour and poured the oil. I can envision her praying while she watched the bread baking in the oven. She exemplifies an overcomer by surviving a famine, not because of a big bank account, but through unwavering faith and complete obedience.

Her faith was so strong that the flour and oil never ran out until the Lord sent rain on the land. Her sacrifice was so monumental that it is recorded for eternity. Her red dress prayer not only removed any fear she had of starvation, but also blessed the man of God and saved her family. We, too, are called to make sacrifices that will eternally impact our families, communities and even the world. We are called to give all so others can see Christ in us and glorify our Father in heaven.

Lord, so many people have made sacrifices for me over the years. You have sacrificed everything (even Your life) so I can live eternally. Thank You for that sacrifice that I will never be able to repay. I want to follow Your example of true sacrifice. Humble me through Your Holy Spirit so I, too, can offer up my red dress or red tie to bless someone.

Chapter 8: Prayer Conquers Fear

Fear immobilizes us. It will rip our hearts from our bodies so we are weakened physically, emotionally and spiritually. Sometimes it comes at once in full force and we are crippled instantaneously. Other times, it oozes in to our lives through nervousness and anxiety.

> "Say to them that are of a fearful heart, be strong, fear not: behold, your God will come with vengeance, even God with a recompense; He will come and save you."
>
> (Isaiah 35:4, KJV)

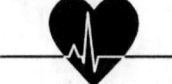

Fear renders us helpless and hopeless so that we cannot think, move, or see all the possibilities before us. It usually shows up in situations in which we have no control. Fear is like a virus. It spreads and infects anyone and everyone without their consent. Fear never ask for permission. Instead, it permeates everywhere and tries to eradicate joy, confidence, and peace.

Fear held my family hostage while on a fun-filled family getaway. We were in the Poconos (Pennsylvania) and my daughters decided to do a rope climbing course. My husband went with them, and for the first ten minutes, everything was going great. My oldest daughter became courageous and started to go higher and higher, quickly leaving her dad behind. She was having so much fun that her face lit up. My maternal instincts were screaming, "Be careful!" but I remained silent and kept on videotaping her. She was in control initially, and walking the tight ropes gracefully as if her feet were planted on solid ground.

All of a sudden, she stopped and became frozen in time and space. Her legs started shaking from side to side. Elevated about three to four stories and harnessed only with a rope. My daughter became immobilized by fear. My husband and I saw the change in her mannerisms, almost at the same time. Her expression changed from laughter and smiles to one of absolute terror. I did not see a catalyst for the transformation, but it was clear that our fun-filled activity had become a nightmare. I did not know what to do being several feet below her, so I began to pray silently while I watched her.

I was on the ground looking up and giving her encouragement to come down on her own. I was trying to stay calm, even though my heart was also crippled with fear. I tried telling her to put one foot in front of the other, but no matter what I said, my daughter refused to move forward. The look on her face made it clear that she no longer had the desire to take another step. All the vigor and energy she had just moments before vanished and she was left with only angst. My daughter was swaying several feet in the sky, preventing others from climbing and maneuvering through the ropes course.

I was yelling up to her while my husband started climbing toward her. He was moving as fast as possible on the swaying ropes, but it felt like an eternity. I was telling him to hurry, while telling my daughter not to let go of the ropes. One of the workers, realizing that things were getting serious, began climbing the ropes toward my daughter. However, due to his parental determination to save our baby girl, my husband (with less climbing experience) got to her first. Just as her legs slipped, my husband was able to grab her and wrap his arms around her. I said a prayer of thanksgiving while finally breathing a sigh of relief.

Fear had taken away my daughter's joy for about fifteen minutes. When my husband and daughter made it to the bottom of the trail, I hugged her so tight that we could barely breathe. Everyone around us was clapping and saying "great job" to her and my husband. We

Overcomer

started walking toward the exit because I wanted to get as far away from the ropes course as possible. My heart was still pounding and I could

> Her confidence screamed "I was born an overcomer and nothing will stop me!"

see my hands slightly shaking from nervousness.

My daughter, on the other hand, was obviously over the horror. She smiled up at me and said, "Maybe I will try again tomorrow." Her confidence screamed "I was born an overcomer and nothing will stop me!" Her resilience was impressive and admirable. Her comments reminded me of what Jesus said, "Assuredly, I say to you, unless you are converted and become as little children, you will by no means enter the kingdom of heaven." (Matthew 18:3, NKJV).

God encourages us to be like children. He wants us to let go of our anxieties and trust Him. He wants us to rely on Him completely, even when we stumble and fall. He wants us to quickly get up and try again tomorrow. A child is usually more eager to try again after being defeated than adults are. We typically internalize our failures and make them bigger than they really are. In the presence of fear, we lose sight of who we are and who Christ is enabling us to be.

Fear can be crippling in all aspects of our lives – personally, professionally, spiritually, etc. It can be triggered by anything and anyone, at any time. Most people's confidence comes from being in a position of control. When we are not in control and things fall apart, we become fearful and anxious. The Bible says that "God hath not given us the spirit of fear; but of power, and of love, and of a sound mind" (2 Timothy 1:7, KJV). Since fear is not from God, it must be from the devil. Despite knowing this, we still struggle with overcoming fear.

I remember having the same reaction - racing heart beats, sweaty palms, and churning stomach - in a business meeting that I felt watching my oldest daughter on that ropes course. I had those feelings because the atmosphere in the meeting room was toxic. The leader on the phone was being hostile and aggressive toward a team member. Some of the other leaders attempted to calm the storm to no avail. Although the belligerent words were not directed at me, I was overwhelmed by their impact.

Overcomer

There was no reason to be fearful in a business meeting, but I could not control being afraid in that moment. I was overwhelmed by the spirit of evil and hate in the room. The leaders were yelling and screaming at each other. Profanity was being spewed from their mouths and you could cut the tension in the room with a knife.

In the midst of the chaos, God said to me, "Pray." I was not sure what words to say until Isaiah 43:1 flowed from my heart. I prayed, "Lord remove the spirit of fear from me. You have said to me, 'Do not fear, for I have redeemed you; I have summoned you by name; you are mine'" (Isaiah 43:1, KJV). These were the words I needed to uplift my spirit. Prayer is the tool we have to counteract negativity and overcome the spirit of fear.

Almost immediately, it was like a light switch was flipped on in the conference room. My fear disappeared and a big smile took residence on my face. Those words became light in the midst of darkness. They gave breath to a suffocating spirit. Those words brought peace into a turbulent and tense situation. They also reminded me of the Bible's warning, "Be not overcome of evil, but overcome evil with good." (Romans 12:21, KJV). I was able to experience the spirit of power, love, and of a sound mind by using good words to overcome evil words.

In our most fearful moments, we can always stand on the Word and be confident in God. We can always pray when our stomachs are in knots, our knees are knocking, and we feel anxiety kicking in. Singing praises to reduce despair and unlock our confidence is also a powerful tool I have begun to harness. Once hope is unlocked, doubt has to depart from our hearts. Faith and fear are like light and darkness. They cannot co-exist in the same time and place. Where there is fear, there is no faith. Where there is faith, there is no fear. Since God does not give us a spirit of fear, it should not take over our lives.

I once heard a pastor say, "We should run toward our fear." Doubt tells us our goals are impossible and that we should run in the opposite direction. Whenever we become anxious and get the inclination to run away, we should pray and ask God to help us run toward our fears. When we run toward our fears, we often learn that the giant we are facing is not as big as we anticipated. This knowledge gives us courage to fight our current battles and strengthens us for future wars.

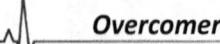 *Overcomer*

I had to be reminded in that business meeting that giants can be slayed if we put on the whole armor of God. On the other hand, my daughter knew this instinctively, which is why she said, "Maybe I will try it again tomorrow," after her terrifying experience. We all have a choice, whether surrounded by the darts of the devil or on a tight rope several feet in the sky - we can let fear conquer us, or we can conquer and overcome fear through prayer.

 *We all have fears. Whether it's fear of heights, public speaking, spiders, meeting new people, etc., fear often steals our joy and limits our achievements. But, I want to proclaim - no more! I will no longer allow my doubts and anxiety to slow me down or stop me. I know, Lord, that fear does not come from You. I will be bold in all situations by remembering and standing on Your Word.*

Chapter 9: Breakthrough Prayer

Pray. Pray. Pray. We have heard people say, "Pray and God will answer." Have you been praying, but to no avail? Have you been praying, but no breakthrough yet? Are you on the brink of death, despair or a nervous breakdown, and need a lifeline?

> "For ye have need of patience, that, after ye have done the will of God, ye might receive the promise."
>
> (Hebrews 10:36, KJV)

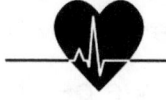

Some of us have been in situations in which we pray for a breakthrough with our whole heart. We pray earnestly, sacrifice meals through fasting, and daily meditate on God's Word. Our desire is for God to instantaneously answer our prayers the way we would like them answered. Many of us think that God's immediate response is all that we need. But no, I have learned that what we really need is to get to know God better and understand *His* ways.

We often treat God like a genie in a bottle, but He, unlike a genie, doesn't always answer our prayers right away. As Christians living in a microwave society, we tend to forget that God does not work on demand. Most of us expect things to be fast and ready now. We have fast food, fast cars, on demand movies, and high-speed internet. We live our lives in a fast-paced manner. Therefore, it is no surprise that we expect God's response to our needs to be expeditious. We want immediate gratification and substantial returns for minimal prayer investment. So, when some of us have to wait for God's answers, we begin to question His ability to meet our needs.

Now just to be clear, "Nothing is impossible with God" (Luke 1:37, KJV). If He chooses, He could answer our prayers before we pray or right after we say amen (Isaiah 65:24, KJV). God has quickly answered prayers in my life and in Biblical stories. 1 Kings 17:21-22 (NKJV) says, "And he stretched himself out on the child three times, and cried out to the Lord and said, "O Lord my God, I pray, let this child's soul come back to him." Then the Lord heard the voice of Elijah; and the soul of the child came back to him, and he revived."

These verses recap Elijah befriending a widow and her son. The widow's son became ill and died. When Elijah prayed for the child's life to return to him, God answered

Elijah's prayer right away. God, being Sovereign, chooses how and when to respond to our requests. There are times when He answers immediately after one petition and other times He remains silent in spite of many prayers.

In Daniel, chapters 9 and 10 (KJV), Daniel prayed to God for the interpretation of his vision and for Israel, who continued to sin, despite being in captivity. The angel of God appeared to Daniel twenty-one days after he began praying. The angel told Daniel that God decided to answer his prayers as soon as he began to pray, however, Satan delayed God's messenger. Satan is pursuing us with the same vigor as he did Daniel. He is hindering us and God's timely response to our prayers.

In addition to Satan's evil plot, there are other reasons for delays in getting answers to our prayers. Some of these setbacks are divinely ordained for our spiritual well-being and growth. Although we want to get to our final destination quickly, growth takes time. It takes time to transition from a dreamer to a dream maker or from a survivor to an overcomer. During this season, we get to know ourselves much better and hear God clearer when He speaks to us.

It is commonly said that God has three answers to all prayers. Those answers are, "Yes," "No," and "Wait." When we pray and God says "Yes," we often rejoice and move forward. We rarely stop to wonder why He said "Yes." God often says "Yes" to us so we can say "Yes" to those around us. He blesses us so we can be a blessing to others. The Bible says, "While you are enriched in everything for all liberality, which causes thanksgiving through us to God." (2 Corinthians 9:11, NKJV).

More often than not, we take the "Yes" from God--a new job, physical healing, or that perfect spouse--and we keep the blessings for ourselves. To truly experience the fullness of God's affirmation, we need to share what we have and bless others. Imagine the joy we would experience if we used the increase from a new job to assist a family struggling financially!

Or what if we openly shared how God delivered us so others might be able to experience that same deliverance and get their long awaited breakthrough? God expects us to do more than just rise from our knees and say "Thank you" or "Amen" after hearing "Yes." He expects us to give back. Unfortunately, we usually don't stop to think of others. We just speed on from "Yes" to self-indulgence.

When we pray and God says "No," we become like a two-year-old child. It is very difficult to hear the word "No" regardless of our age. When we hear "No," we either throw a tantrum, have a pity party, or we proclaim, "God, you are not my friend anymore." But, God never contradicts Himself - if we truly believe that, then there must be a reason for the answer "No."

I remember a pastor saying, "When God says 'No,' there is a bigger 'Yes' in store for us. Jesus said 'No' to the healing of Lazarus because He had resurrection in store for him." Are you praying for a healing when God is planning for a resurrection? In Lazarus' case, Jesus' initial "No" meant temporary sleep. However, Jesus' subsequent "Yes" meant a divine resurrection; a resurrection that has transcended through time and generations.

It is so easy to focus on the "No" and fall into a spiritual funk. If we turn our focus to what is beyond the "No," we will experience God like never before. God will bring to life what we consider dead and will make the impossible possible. He will turn sorrow and weeping into joy as we behold the grandeur of His "Yes."

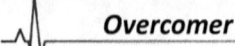

Our reaction to God's "Yes" or "No" is almost immediate, a burst of joy or sadness. Our reaction to God's "Wait" is usually one of lingering doubt. For those of us who are impatient, the "Wait" also causes us to second guess God. We become skeptical about His love and our relationship with Him.

Skepticism as to whether or not we heard God's response correctly, whether God's answer will come in our lifetime, if His answer will be contrary to our wishes, or whether we will get the breakthrough we have been praying for, for so long. Doubt is real. It can be a strong adversary or impenetrable wall. However, disbelief never changes God's answer of "Wait." It only causes turmoil and hinders our spiritual growth.

We have a choice during the waiting period - we can either be still or move forward outside of God's will. In my experience, going outside of the will of God always ends in disaster. Therefore, I have learned to wait. I have also chosen to pray and praise while waiting. What do you do during the waiting period?

Perspective is everything, and praise fosters a spiritual mindset even in dire situations. Prayer and praise give us hope when our situations remain stagnant or get worse. God does not want us to lose hope during the waiting period. So if you are on the verge of giving up, do not quit.

We can't overcome if we quit, so prayer and perseverance is the key.

I admonish everyone who is contemplating quitting to hold on for a little longer. We may not see what the future holds, but we know that God holds the future in His hands. When we decide to give up, we never experience the full manifestation of God's power in our lives. Remember, failure is never an option. We can't overcome if we quit, so prayer and perseverance is the key.

The "Wait" is not to cause our faith to waiver, but rather to build our confidence in God. It is to have faith when everything around goes contrary to what God has promised us. Remember, "Faith is the substance of things hoped for, the evidence of things not seen" (Hebrews 11:1, NKJV). This means that we have to believe in a better and brighter tomorrow, even though today may be our worst day. We have to hold on to our dreams and aspirations and never give up on them regardless of the struggles we face each day. Even though we cannot see

God, we have to believe that He exists and His promises will always come through.

It is challenging to hold on to our faith in God while being bombarded by pain, adversity, poverty, etc. Most of us do not want to suffer or endure the storms of life. We want the answers to our prayers now. However, perseverance always pays off when we pray. There may be no breakthrough yet, but I can guarantee that it is coming. I have this assurance because after almost three years of praying for a less stressful job, my breakthrough came right on time. I cannot tell you when, where, or how yours will come, but I am confident that it will come to pass.

God never leaves "the righteous forsaken or His seed begging bread" (Psalms 37:25, KJV). While we wait, we have to "hold fast the confession of our hope without wavering, for He who promised is faithful" (Hebrews 10:23, NKJV). We cannot become slack in our prayer life and we cannot let our faith waiver. When we cannot find the words to pray, we can sing praises to God. Praise God for who He is and proclaim His promises.

Because of who God is, we can breakthrough any wall or obstacle. Our breakthroughs may not have broken through yet, but when they do, all of our tears will turn into laughter. We will not remember the "Wait." We will only testify about God's miracles and how He strengthened our faith. Therefore, let us not cry and complain like those who have no hope, but continue to pray, pray and pray because a breakthrough is around the corner.

Jesus, I need a breakthrough; but more than anything, I need You. I have been waiting a long time for my prayers to be answered. As I wait, I am learning that You know what's best for me. My timing is often different from Yours. But, Your will and my willingness to obey is the perfect union. Thank You for this lesson and the many others You are teaching me during this waiting period.

Overcomer

Chapter 10: Praying Through Scriptures

Born to be late. I was running late for work again, even though I woke up early. My daughter cried during the entire ride to school. I walked into work to face issue after issue and I did not get the chance to eat lunch until 2:30 p.m. It was a frustrating day from start to end.

> "For we wrestle not against flesh and blood, but against principalities, against powers, against the rulers of the darkness of this world, against spiritual wickedness in high places."
>
> (Ephesians 1:12, KJV)

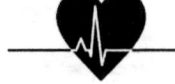

As I laid in bed that night, wondering why my day was so horrible, it came to me as plain as day: I did not pray when I woke up that morning. I left the house in a hurry without saying a word of prayer. That morning, I knew I needed to pray. But I struggled to utter the words that were trapped in my heart. I went through the day without speaking to God.

Many things kept me from praying - too busy rushing around, too tired from not getting enough sleep, too overwhelmed by life, and too burdened by sins. I cannot blame anyone or anything for my disobedience and refusal to pray that morning except me. When the Holy

Spirit gives specific directions and we disobey, there are always consequences.

I made a conscious decision that I didn't have enough time to pray, but in the end, the consequence was separation from God and lack of direction for the day. Sometimes the ramification of defiance is immediate - like having bad day - and other times it's delayed - like losing our eternal salvation. We rarely think of all the consequences when we make certain decisions.

Nevertheless, there are repercussions when we go outside of God's will. To avoid them, we have to seek God first and continually talk to Him. There are many ways to communicate with each other such as through words, body language, and even silence. However, communicating with our Heavenly Father requires prayer - prayers of humility, prayers of transparency, and prayers of the heart.

Many people think they cannot pray unless they are in the "right" physical posture. However, posture is only a piece of the puzzle. We can choose to close our eyes or keep them open. We can bend our knees or lay prostrate before God. We can whisper or cry out to Him. We can pray while we are standing, running, or laying down. God sees past our stance and looks upon the heart.

A sincere prayer requires a pure heart and having an undefiled heart is critical to one's salvation. Knowing this, the devil does whatever he can and uses whoever is available to prevent us from communing with God. I have found that whenever I try to pray, the phone rings, my kids want my attention, or there is some other type of distraction.

Sometimes when I kneel to pray, my mind wanders to insignificant and ungodly things. Nevertheless as children of God, we must purpose in our hearts and minds to pray always. When we do not pray, we enter the danger zone - the zone that causes us to rely on ourselves or others rather than on God. Are you living in the danger zone?

The Bible is clear that we should pray without ceasing (1 Thessalonians 5:16, KJV). For those who sometimes struggle to pray, there are many published techniques. One technique that has always resonated with me is taking a scripture in the Bible and praying through it verse by verse. It could be your favorite scripture or one that you struggle to fully understand. One of my favorites is Psalms 62 (KJV) which says:

> **Verse 1: "Truly my soul waiteth upon God: from him cometh my salvation."** *Lord, when everything is rushed and fast paced, it is so difficult to wait and be patient. I know in my heart You have already taken care of every situation. Teach me Lord to be patient, to be confident in Your saving grace, and to truly wait on You.*
>
> **Verse 2: "He only is my rock and my salvation; He is my defense; I shall not be greatly moved."** *Jesus, You are my protector when I am being attacked by others. You are my all in all. No matter what life throws at me, I will not run away. I will stand up. On the job and at home, I will stand up and will not be moved.*
>
> **Verse 3: "How long will ye imagine mischief against a man? Ye shall be slain all of you: as a bowing wall shall ye be, and as a tottering fence."** *I know my enemies want to destroy me. The devil wants me to doubt You. God, You have overcome the devil. I know no weapon formed against me shall prosper. Whatever trial I face will help me grow closer to You.*

Overcomer

You said in Your Word that when I am weak, You are strong.

Verse 4: "They only consult to cast him down from his Excellency: they delight in lies: they bless with their mouth, but they curse inwardly. Selah." *Lord, remove the scales from my eyes, so I may see and discern those who are for me and those who are against me. Help me not to delight in lies, but to discern righteousness and meditate on things that are pure, true, and kind. I do not want to be a hypocrite who blesses others with my mouth, but curses them in my heart.*

Verse 5: "My soul, wait thou only upon God; for my expectation is from him." *Teach me to wait on You. Teach me to rely completely on You. Everything I have comes from You. My expectation is in You, Lord. Teach me to trust that Your timing is always right. It's hard to wait patiently, but I know that Godly things come to those who wait on You.*

Verse 6: "He only is my rock and my salvation: He is my defense; I shall not be moved." *You are the solid rock on which I stand. It is commonly said that if you cannot stand for something, then you will fall for* anything. By Your grace, I will stand for You and will not lean on my own understanding. I will not be afraid because You are my defense and You have a hedge around me.

> When we get to heaven, overcomers will hear "Well done good and faithful servant."

Verse 7: "In God is my salvation and my glory: the rock of my strength, and my refuge, is in God." Lord, my hope is in You. I believe that soon, and very soon, You will return to take Your children home. When we get to heaven, overcomers will hear "Well done good and faithful servant." I pray that all my loved ones and the person reading this book now will be among those You welcome with open arms and these words of affirmation.

Verse 8: "Trust in him at all times; ye people, pour out your heart before him: God is a refuge for us. Selah." I am learning to trust You more every day. It is so sweet to take You at Your Word. When I am in fearful situations, help me to rely on You. When I am in lonely situations, help me to feel Your presence.

Every morning when I wake up, Lord, help me to surrender all to You.

Verse 9: "Surely men of low degree are vanity, and men of high degree are a lie: to be laid in the balance, they are altogether lighter than vanity." Lord help me not to focus on this world. Everything in this world is vanity. Keep me focused on the one thing that is everlasting. Keep me focused on You, Lord. I am nothing compared to Your glory and I desire nothing but to have You in charge of my life.

Verse 10: "Trust not in oppression, and become not vain in robbery: if riches increase, set not your heart upon them." I know that no matter what I attain on this earth, it is worthless if I do not have You. Teach me to focus on You and not to be materialistic. I don't want to be un-ethical, immoral, or pursue evil in order to gain riches. Help me to pursue righteousness always.

Verse 11: "God hath spoken once; twice have I heard this; that power belongeth unto God." All power belongs to You, God. You are awesome and there is no one like You. You created this world out of nothing. You spoke and it all came into existence.

Your words are life and power. Through Your words, there is joy, peace, and hope.

Verse 12: "Also unto thee, O Lord, belongeth mercy: for thou renderest to every man according to his work." *Thank You, Lord for Your mercy. You repeatedly forgive me when I deserve punishment. You bless me beyond measure and consistently fill my food basket. You are so amazing that You shine on the just and the unjust. You provide for those who love You and those who confess they hate You. Your faithfulness is beyond words. I thank You, Lord, for loving a sinner like me.*

Praying through Scriptures is like breathing in fresh air after being trapped inside a smoky or dust filled room. It allows me to hold on when I am losing my grip on God. Prayer is like music at a party helping me to celebrate overcoming fear, negativity, and past failures. Praying through Scriptures ensures peace and joy despite spiritual battles. It strengthens me as I wait on God's will to be done.

If you are waiting on your breakthrough or you are struggling, hold on and pray. I encourage you to take Psalms 62, or your favorite Bible verses, and pray through them. I promise the verses will come alive. Your prayer life will be revived as you meditate on each word. I strongly recommend practicing this "praying through Scripture" technique. Prayer is not natural, but it's very necessary. By overcoming our natural tendencies not to pray, we will be uplifted in the Spirit and will begin to enjoy the time spent with Jesus.

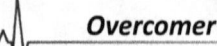

Thank You, Lord, for helping me learn different ways to communicate with You. Sometimes, it is difficult to find the words to express how I am feeling. Praying through Scripture is so refreshing. Remind me to pray each moment of the day. I want to draw closer to You and fully experience the power that comes with prayer. Prayer has saved many lives including mine. Thank You Jesus for the gift of prayer and for sacrificing everything so we can have eternal life.

Closing Thoughts

Prayer is not a natural reaction to our daily circumstances. For this reason, prayer can be challenging and even awkward at times. It is critical to understand that struggling to pray is not a negative reflection on ourselves. However when we choose not to pray, we are ultimately choosing to leave God out of our lives.

Prayer is a journey - it is a transformational experience. God calls us to be people of prayer, both in our personal lives and within our churches. Both personal and communal prayers unleash God's power and reveal His faithfulness. He is faithful to me and to everyone who cries out to Him. I hope that you will continue to experience His faithfulness and never doubt that prayer works; prayer changes people and circumstances.

I encourage you, in this very moment, to reflect on your journey - the highs and lows, the joys and pains, the times that you've been victorious and the times that you've felt defeated. Everything that you have gone through has a divine purpose, and God will continue to reveal His purpose for your life as your continue to prayerfully seek His will.

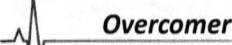
Overcomer

Prayer is powerful. It erases past mistakes and validates future aspirations. More importantly, it draws us closer to God so we can reflect His image. God's desire is for us to be like Him in every way so we can overcome this world. He promised, "To him that overcometh will I give to eat of the tree of life, which is in the midst of the paradise of God" (Revelation 2:7, KJV). Keep praying! Your eternal reward will be so sweet.

Overcomer

Preview of Book Two
Excerpt from the Chapter: Jump

Many people are imprisoned with thoughts of hurting themselves on a daily basis. Some are able to ignore these suicidal thoughts, while others are trapped by the constant surge to end their lives. Suicide and related topics of self-mutilation remain tabooed in our society.

However, according to the Centers for Disease Control and Prevention (CDC), suicide is the 10th leading cause of death and is one of just three leading causes that are on the rise (2016). This crisis requires that we identify and acknowledge when our family members, friends, neighbors, and colleagues are living in a state of hopelessness.

No one is immune to the spirit of darkness, and I have experienced the devastating grip of this spirit. I recall my family and I were riding the Long Island Ferry to Manhattan during last summer. The ferry was a melting pot of native New Yorkers and tourists from all over the world. Everyone eagerly positioned themselves close to the railings on the ferry to see the sights.

The view was spectacular. The Manhattan skyline glistened with bright white lights. The lights reflected on the dark blue-gray water while the sun was setting on the horizon. The magnificent orange and red-glazed shadow of the sun wrapped behind the Statue of Liberty like a well-tailored suit.

Like many of the bright-eyed tourists, I leaned over the ferry railings. The tapestry of nature embracing one of the world's famous symbols of freedom was breathtaking. I was mesmerized by the sight and elated by the expression of joy on both my daughters' faces. Suddenly in my mind, I heard the word, "Jump." I froze in that moment. My body did not move, but my mind was racing fast.

My eyes tried to focus on the rushing water and waves beneath the boat. I was captivated by the water's ferociousness and then I heard the words again. "Jump! Just Jump!" I then foresaw my body slipping beneath the rushing water. This vision frightened me so much that I quickly backed away from the railing.

My focus was no longer on Lady Liberty, but on the floor of the ferry. In a daze, I sat down on the bench and reflected on hearing the same voice earlier in the day. It tried to persuade me to jump from the second floor of the mall. When I heard the voice at the mall, I thought it was a random, silly thought, so I brushed it off and went about my business.

The devilish directions on the ferry made me realize that this was not simply me hearing things. I was not out of my mind and I was not hallucinating. I was urged to jump to my death twice in one day, which was perplexing to me. As a child of God, how could suicidal thoughts even enter my mind?

About The Author

Bridgette Bastien is a prayer enthusiast and the author of the *Prayer Saved My Life* series. Writing a book was never on her bucket list, until she was snatched from the jaws of death. After going through that experience, Bastien has a reignited burning desire to share the transformational power of prayer and to celebrate the saving grace of God with others. She feasts on the Bible and, according to her daughters, "She has playdates with her prayer group three times per day."

Bastien has published several children's books written by her daughters. She was a research chemist early in her career, holds a Master's degree in Strategy and Marketing from the Wharton School of Business - University of Pennsylvania, and is now a marketing professional. Bastien lives in Massachusetts with her family. She loves traveling the world, eating spicy foods, and basking in the warmth of her family and friends' love. Learn more at:

- www.prayersavedmylife.com
- Facebook.com/prayersavedmylife
- Instagram.com/prayersavedmylife
- Twitter.com/prayersavedmy

Special thanks to my editors for your prayers and talent:

Lahai McKinnie holds a B.A. in Journalism and a Masters in Social Work. She has over 16 years of editorial experience including working at *Adventist Review*. McKinnie enjoys sewing and reading. She lives with her family in Delaware. Her favorite scripture is *"For I am persuaded that neither death nor life, nor angels nor principalities nor powers, nor things present nor things to come, nor height nor depth, nor any other created thing, shall be able to separate us from the love of God which is in Christ Jesus our Lord"* (Romans 8:38-39 NKJV).

Fiona Harewood is a published author and motivational speaker. Her book - *I Did It, You Can, Too!* - is part of the Philadelphia School District summer reading list. Harewood has a Master's in Public Policy from Drexel University and works with the Federal Government. She lives in Philadelphia with her family and is a member of Mizpah SDA Church. Harewood has a passion for writing, working with children, and using her gifts to glorify God. She often reflects on Proverbs 31:30 (NKJV) which says *"Charm is deceitful and beauty is passing, but a woman who fears the Lord, she shall be praised."*

Kerrie Howard is a dedicated pastor's wife and stay-at-home-mother of three. In the midst of these roles, she continues to pursue her passions for writing and editing. She has a degree in English from Worcester State University and is working on a Master's degree in Publishing from The George Washington University. Above all, her desire is to serve her Lord and Savior, Jesus Christ, in everything that she does. Most recently, the scripture that says *"Be still and know that I am God,"* (Psalm 46:10, NKJV) has become very meaningful to Kerrie; she has found peace in stillness and joy in the simplicities of life.

Overcomer

PRAYER Can Save Your Life

www.ingramcontent.com/pod-product-compliance
Lightning Source LLC
LaVergne TN
LVHW021407080426
835508LV00020B/2478